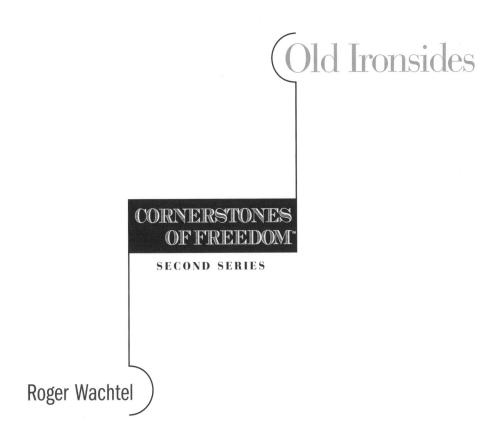

Old Ironsides

CORNERSTONES OF FREEDOM™

SECOND SERIES

Roger Wachtel

Children's Press®
A Division of Scholastic Inc.
New York • Toronto • London • Auckland • Sydney
Mexico City • New Delhi • Hong Kong
Danbury, Connecticut

Photographs © 2003: Bridgeman Art Library International Ltd., London/New York: 11, 44 bottom (Christie's Images), 8 (Philip Mould, Historical Portraits Ltd, London, UK), 35 right (Rafael Valls Gallery, London, UK), 15 (Victoria & Albert Museum, London), 39, 45 center (Ken Welsh), 6; Corbis Images: 21, 22, 30 (Bettmann), 24 (Ray Krantz), 3 (Tracy Lee), 10 (MAPS.com), 20 right (Museum of the City of New York), 5 (Gianni Dagli Orti), 16 (Patrick Ward), 13, 20 left, 31, 44 top right; North Wind Picture Archives: 40, 41 (N. Carter), cover top, cover bottom, 4, 7 bottom, 18, 27, 32, 34, 35 left, 36, 44 top left, 45 bottom, 45 top; Stock Montage, Inc.: 7 top.

XNR Productions: Map on page 28

Library of Congress Cataloging-in-Publication Data

Wachtel, Roger.
    Old Ironsides / Roger Wachtel.
        p. cm.—(Cornerstones of freedom. Second series)
Summary: Discusses the history and exploits of the U.S.S. *Constitution*, or "Old Ironsides," a frigate built in the late eighteenth century to fight the pirates of the Barbary States that still floats today.
Includes bibliographical references and index.
    ISBN 0-516-24207-5
    1. Constitution (Frigate)—Juvenile literature. [1. Constitution (Frigate)] I. Title. II. Series.
VA65.C7 W33 2003
359.3'22'0973—dc21

2002009032

CHILDREN'S PRESS, AND CORNERSTONES OF FREEDOM™, and associated logos are trademarks and or registered trademarks of Grolier Publishing Co., Inc. SCHOLASTIC and associated logos are trademarks and or registered trademarks of Scholastic Inc.

1 2 3 4 5 6 7 8 9 10 R 12 11 10 09 08 07 06 05 04 03

A T THE BEGINNING OF the twenty-first century, the United States maintains what many consider to be the most powerful navy in the world. Almost 600,000 sailors and marines serve on more than 140 ships and 100 submarines. A dozen of the ships are aircraft carriers, which are as large as some small cities. The navy's weapons are very advanced, requiring highly technical training to operate. Some are able to hit targets hundreds of miles away. There is almost no place on earth out of reach of the U.S. Navy.

★ ★ ★ ★

Despite all this amazing power, the navy also maintains one very unusual ship. It is made of wood. It requires no computers. It rarely leaves dock, and when it does, it does so with sails flown from its three masts. It is hundreds of years old, but still on active duty. Several times throughout its life, the government has decided it is no longer necessary and they thought it should be destroyed. Each time, there was an outcry from the citizens of the United States, unwilling to allow their most famous fighting ship, the USS *Constitution*, "Old Ironsides," to be forgotten.

THE EARLY NAVY

It is hard to believe today, but there was a time when the United States had no navy. Before 1776, the United States

Superior fighting ships and fine sailors made the British navy among the most powerful in the world during the 1700s.

* * * *

In the earliest years of the United States, the government had to rely on merchant ships rigged with guns for protection.

did not exist. The country was then part of Great Britain, which had one of the most powerful navies in the world. When the Americans began to fight for their independence from Britain, the colonists were at a great disadvantage on the seas. They only had merchant vessels meant for transporting goods so the colonists could trade with other parts of the world. They were outstanding ships, but no match for the British navy, which had large, powerful ships with cannons

Eighteenth and nineteenth century warships sometimes carried between forty and sixty guns, some of which could fire shells up to two-thirds of a mile.

capable of reducing a merchant ship to pieces in a matter of minutes. The Colonial government was forced to use **priva-teers,** privately owned warships, for protection. Congress did eventually create a Continental Navy, but many of the navy's ships were just merchants with guns attached to them.

Eventually, the navy grew to sixty ships and produced one of the American Revolution's most famous heroes. Captain John Paul Jones was in command of the *Bonhomme Richard* as it battled the heavily armed British ship *Serapis.* At one point in the battle, the ships got very close. Their **rigging,** the ropes and cables that control the masts and sails, became entangled. They were so close that their cannons actually touched. Jones's ship was outgunned and badly damaged, and *Serapis* demanded his surrender. "I have not yet begun to fight!" was his reply. Though the *Bonhomme Richard* eventually sank, it was only after Jones had already defeated and captured *Serapis*. The proud tradition of the U.S. Navy had begun, but still had a long way to go.

When the Revolution was over, decisions had to be made about how to defend

When Captain John Paul Jones's *Bonhomme Richard* defeated the British ship *Serapis*, Jones became the United States' first naval hero.

At times during their battle, the *Bonhomme Richard* and the *Serapis* fought so closely that their rigging became entangled.

Future president Thomas Jefferson feared that creating a navy would give the United States the means to control foreign lands, just as the British had done to the colonists.

the new nation. The war with Britain had been very expensive, and the cost of independence was high. The country was deeply in debt. Many important citizens, among them future president Thomas Jefferson, felt that there should be no military whatsoever. A navy, he argued, might encourage imperialism, the practice of controlling foreign lands for a country's own benefit. That, Jefferson said, was what they had just fought against.

Regardless of whether it was the right thing to do, the new nation simply could not afford to operate a navy, so it began selling off its ships. The last vessel from the Continental Navy, the *Alliance,* was auctioned for $26,000 in 1785. Just because the new government could not afford a navy, however, did not mean it was unnecessary. Soon it would become obvious that American citizens on the high seas were in danger. They were unprotected, and something would have to be done.

DANGER OFF THE BARBARY STATES

Even before the colonies won their independence from Britain, they had many trading partners around the world. Merchant sailors sailed back and forth to Europe and Africa and south into the Caribbean Sea. They left with raw materials and goods that were only available in North America. Then they sold them or traded them for goods available in other parts of the world. This was very profitable for the countries involved, but it often came at a heavy price.

THE BARBARY STATES

The countries along the coast of North Africa on the Mediterranean Sea were once known as the Barbary States. Today this area is the northern coast of the countries of Morocco, Algeria, Tunisia, and Libya. They were called the Barbary States because people such as the North Africans, who had once lived on the edge of the Roman Empire, were called *barbari*, from the Latin word for "foreigner."

Trading with the countries on the Mediterranean Sea had always been dangerous. Since the 1500s, the Barbary States had attacked ships from other nations. They were ruled by **despots,** all-powerful rulers, who ran corrupt governments. **Piracy** was their major source of income. They hired sea raiders, called **corsairs,** to harass, attack, and even capture ships and crews. The ships' cargoes were taken, and often sailors were held for large ransoms. There was even a religious organization in France dedicated to raising funds for the ransom of sailors captured by the Barbary pirates.

10

* * * *

To avoid this, many countries began paying **tributes** to the Barbary States. A tribute is a fee one country pays to another not to attack its ships. Even powerful nations such as Britain and France, which had navies large enough to defeat the corsairs, found it less expensive simply to pay tributes than to engage in sea battles with the raiders.

After the colonies won their independence from Britain, U.S. captains began to have problems with the pirates. Before the Revolutionary War, Britain had paid the tributes that protected all their ships, including those of the colonies. Now that the United States was independent, American

Attacks by corsairs could be so costly that even powerful countries like Britain and France paid tributes rather than do battle with them.

ships were on their own. British businessmen were very happy about American ships being attacked. Their former countrymen were now competing with them. Anything that hurt the competition was good for British merchants.

Other dangers existed as well. There were pirates in other waters attacking American ships and calling for tributes. In the late 1700s, Britain and France were at war, and France sometimes treated U.S. vessels as if they were still under British control. French ships would often attack U.S. ships and impress their crews, or force them to serve in the French navy. The British navy stopped American ships with goods meant for France, and French ships stopped American ships with goods bound for Britain.

The merchants were fed up. They were losing money, their ships were being destroyed, and American citizens were being captured and killed. Life on the high seas had become too dangerous for U.S. ships. They needed protection. The United States would once again have to build a navy.

THE HUMPHREYS FRIGATES

Even though the need for a navy seemed clear, there was still heated debate over whether to build one. Most of the merchant ships were from the northeastern states. Building a navy powerful enough to protect American ships would require a lot of money that the poor nation did not have. It would require a nationwide tax. In other words, southerners, farmers, and others who had little to do with the sea would be among those paying for the protection of New England businesses. Much of what the ships carried

Since Congress only funded the building of six warships to protect American interests, Secretary of War Henry Knox looked for a design for a ship that would be fast enough and strong enough to battle the country's enemies.

WHAT IS A FRIGATE?

A frigate is a ship that is meant to defend slow or unarmed ships that are vulnerable to attack. Before the USS *Constitution* was built, frigates were often small and considered unimportant. During battles they were frequently assigned to stay to the side, out of battle, and relay messages to crews blinded by gun smoke. Today frigates are very fast and well armed, meant to defend larger ships from attacks by submarines and aircraft. Most of the frigates in the U.S. Navy are now called cruisers.

came from southern farms, but many southerners and others were still against it.

Some people suggested that instead of preparing for war, there was another way to handle the problem. They thought treaties should be negotiated with the hostile countries. A treaty is an agreement between two nations. Often, countries that sign treaties decide to trade with one another rather than go to war.

The Navy Act of March 27, 1794, did finally allocate $688,888.32 to establish a U.S. Navy, but it only called for the building of six frigates. According to the act, even they would be taken out of service if a treaty could be made with the Barbary States. The secretary of war at the time was General Henry Knox. It was his job to make sure the country was properly protected and prepared to go to war, if necessary. Knox was afraid that six ships would not be enough. Britain and France had hundreds. He decided that if six ships were all they would build, they would have to be six very special ships.

Knox consulted with naval officers and shipbuilders. They knew that to battle the pirates, as well as powerful foreign navies, these ships would have to be big enough to outgun their enemies, and fast enough to outrun them. They would have to be unlike any ships that had ever been built—the best of the best. No frigates built up to that time could meet those requirements, so Knox decided to redefine what a frigate was.

After consulting with experts, Knox better understood what he was up against. When ships are designed, many decisions need to be made. Knox knew there would have to be as many guns as possible, but guns meant weight. Twenty-four pound cannons, so named because they fired a 24-pound lead ball, weighed three tons. The guns needed ammunition, enough for multiple battles. Thousands of rounds of ammunition and gunpowder, called **ordnance,** meant several more tons. Guns, of course, were no good without men to fire them. Since each gun required a crew

Frigates like this one had historically been second-rate ships, but Joshua Humphreys' design of the USS *Constitution* established them as among the fastest and strongest on the seas.

★　★　★　★

of twelve, plus food and water for the men, it added tremendous weight. All of this weight slowed the ship down. Yet Knox knew these ships would have to be fast, too. Many people thought it would be impossible to build a ship that could meet these requirements. What builder could design such a ship?

The government did not have to look far. Americans had long been excellent shipbuilders. Their fishing ships were second to none, and their sailing ships were among the fastest of the day. However, they had not built warships

The ribs in a ship's frame were usually two feet apart, but the *Constitution*'s were two inches apart. It was this added strength that earned the ship the nickname, "Old Ironsides."

16

that could compete with those of Britain yet. The goal was to find the right man to design these special ships.

The right man turned out to be Joshua Humphreys. He was a master shipwright from Philadelphia. Shipwrights were very special people. They were part architect, part engineer, part artist, and master carpenter. They had to study charts and tables, passed down from generation to generation, that explained what would and would not work in ship design. It was clear, however, that Humphreys was ready for this job. He even had models already built when Knox contacted him.

Humphreys proposed a ship wider and longer than similar British and French ships. In fact, the *Constitution* was 175 feet (53.3 m) long and 45 feet 2 inches (13.77 m) wide, about 20 feet (6.1 m) longer and 2 to 3 feet (a little less than a meter) wider than the British frigates. The combination of length and width, as well as the shape of the **keel** and **cutwater,** made it much faster than its European counterparts.

Humphreys' design also resulted in a much stronger ship. The beams in the ship's frame, which look like ribs, were about 2 inches (55 millimeters) apart. In frigates of the day the beams were typically *2 feet* (60 cm) apart. This close placement of the beams had the effect of a hull made of solid wood, providing the kind of strength that would earn the *Constitution* the nickname "Old Ironsides."

Finally, Humphreys borrowed an idea from the roofs he had seen on Pennsylvania Dutch farms. He used long interlocking

THE SHIP'S GUNS—NUMBER

The weaponry of ships during the *Constitution's* era was very important. The number of guns a ship carried defined the ship itself. Since the *Constitution* was designed for 44 guns, for example, it is often referred to in older documents by the name *Constitution,* 44. However, the *Constitution* often carried more than 44 cannons, occasionally as many as 60.

★ ★ ★ ★

Hartt Brothers shipyard near Boston, Massachusetts, received the contract to build the *Constitution*, while her sister ships were created at different yards up and down the east coast of the United States.

diagonal beams that connected to the gun decks. That added even more strength and stability. In other ships the biggest guns had to be placed very carefully to prevent what sailors call hogging. Hogging occurs when the part of the ship where the heavy guns are located sits deeper in the water, which slows it down. The added strength of Humphreys' designs also allowed for much larger masts that could support more sails, adding even more speed. It was clear genius.

Eventually, Humphreys' designs were accepted, and contracts to build three ships were awarded to shipyards up and down the eastern coast of the United States. The *Constitution* was to be built in Boston, in the Hartt brothers' shipyard under the guidance of George Claghorne. At the same time, the wood for the ship was collected. Almost 2,000 trees, representing about 60 acres (24 hectares) of forest, would be needed. The trees were cut by hand in many different states. Live oak came from Georgia, pine came from Maine, New Jersey, and South Carolina, and more oak for the deck came from Massachusetts. Humphreys was specific about live oak for his creation. While live oak is very heavy, it is also very hard. It can withstand cannon shot and exposure to salt water for up to fifty years.

Another issue was the new ship's name. Recently appointed secretary of war Timothy Pickering showed a list of possible names to President George Washington in March of 1795. Pickering had talked to several men he admired and developed a list of ten names, five of which the president approved. Honoring the still new document

Secretary of War Timothy Pickering (left) consulted with President George Washington to choose the names of the Humphreys' frigates. *Constitution* is said to have been Washington's favorite name.

establishing the different rights and laws of the United States, the *Constitution* was Washington's favorite. Very soon after, the *Constitution* was painted on the back of the ship, still under construction in Boston.

It took almost three years to build the *Constitution*. Many of its other parts were created during that time as well, including nearly 40 sails of all shapes. This ship would sail with more canvas than any other. The main topsail alone was 80 feet (24.3 m) wide and 50 feet (15.2 m) high and weighed one-half ton. All together, the *Constitution* was equipped with more than an acre of sail. The guns were made in Providence, Rhode Island. The 24-pounders required the largest metal **casting** ever done in America. The copper pieces, nails, and other metal work, including the ship's bell, were made in a shop owned by Paul Revere, who had become famous for alerting the people of Boston that "The British are coming" at the start of the Revolutionary War.

Paul Revere was best known as a patriot, but he was also one of the finest metalsmiths in the country. Revere's shop provided much of the metal for the *Constitution*.

Typical eighteenth-century ships like this one gained much of their speed from the number of sails they were able to use. The *Constitution* had more sail than any ship ever built.

Even with all that work, the *Constitution* still almost was never finished. The Navy Act of 1794 said that if a peace agreement was reached with the Barbary States, the ships would not be built. In March of 1796 a treaty was signed. Under this agreement, American ships would be allowed to travel safely to the Barbary States and trade freely with them. However, many people did not trust the treaties. Since the ships were well on their way to being completed, Congress told President Washington that he could order that the ships be finished. They also said Washington could have more ships built if he felt it necessary. The situation on the seas soon worsened, and it was becoming clear that even the *Constitution* and its sister ships would not be enough.

EARLY FAILURES

Perhaps the *Constitution's* worst day was the day it was supposed to have been launched. By September of 1797, the *Constitution* was the biggest thing on the Boston waterfront. Two of its sister ships, the *United States* and the *Constellation,* had already been launched, and the citizens of Boston, proud of "their" ship, wanted to see it put to sea, as well.

On September 20, at 11:20 A.M., high tide, with the governor of Massachusetts and president of the United States watching, it was time. George Claghorne ordered the crew to knock out the blocks, which would send the *Constitution* down ramps, called ways, to the water. The crowd hushed itself, ready to celebrate the navy's newest ship, but nothing happened. They tried another method to get the *Constitution* going and it did move—27 feet (8.2 m), again well short of the water. The ways had sunk into the mud.

Two days later, after the ways had been raised, the scene was repeated. This time it went 31 feet (9.4 m), almost to the water, before stopping. Embarrassed, Claghorne almost tried to force the *Constitution* into the water, but the likelihood of

CHRISTENING A SHIP

Since sailing is dangerous, sailors are very superstitious. How seamen launch their ships is steeped in tradition. Typically, the ship is blessed, then a woman breaks a bottle of champagne on the bow while pronouncing, "In the name of the United States, I christen thee . . . ," followed by the name of the ship. It is then allowed to slide into the water. That is how *Constitution* was christened, except a navy captain did the honors with a bottle of wine.

The *Constitution* was christened by a ship's captain with a bottle of wine. Today, the honors are typically done by girls or women smashing a bottle of champagne on the bow.

causing damage to the ship was high and he decided against it. Finally, a month later, Claghorne had one of the *Constitution*'s cannons fired to signal that it would be launched at last. After a short ceremony, the *Constitution* slid into the water on October 21, 1797.

The *Constitution*'s first captain, Samuel Nicholson, may not have been the right man for the job. He supervised the building of the ship and spent a lot of time on the docks, yelling at the workers while the ship was under construction. The workers grew to hate him so much that they even denied him the honor of taking the flag aboard when it was finished, as was the custom.

When the ship finally sailed, the crew Nicholson chose performed poorly and they showed little respect for him. Though he had some successes, on some occasions he was not ready to sail when the navy ordered him to. Once, he was a month late carrying out orders! To make things worse, his son, who was on the crew, died of an illness. The ship was in port at the time because Captain Nicholson was under investigation for taking illegal prisoners. Nicholson's son was actually the first casualty recorded in the *Constitution*'s log.

Nicholson feuded with his officers, made several mistakes, and generally served inadequately. On top of that, Congress wanted to know why the *Constitution* had cost $188,000 over the original budget to build. Although the *Constitution* won a few races, it was hard to tell if Humphreys' designs were even successful. In 1801, the *Constitution* returned to Boston for repairs, and Nicholson resigned his command.

DIRECTIONS ABOARD SHIP

The words right and left are not used on board a ship, nor are front or back. Traditionally sailors use unique terms to describe direction at sea. The *bow* is the front of the ship and the *stern* is the rear. The port side is the left side as a sailor looks toward the bow, and starboard side refers to the right side.

THE BARBARY WARS

About that same time, the pasha, or leader, of Tripoli began demanding a significant increase in tribute. The treaty with Algiers had kept things quiet in the Mediterranean, but now that also changed. When President Thomas Jefferson refused to pay the protection money, the pasha responded by having the flagpole of the U.S. **consul** chopped down. War was officially declared, Barbary-style. Soon corsairs were once again attacking American ships.

Angered at the behavior of the Barbary States, Congress began sending larger squadrons to the Mediterranean. In 1803, with Edward Preble in command, the *Constitution* was sent to join them. Once there, it would serve as the **flagship,** with Preble as commodore.

The *Constitution*'s captain won the respect of everyone in the crew after an incident in the Strait of Gibraltar, the entrance to the Mediterranean, where he came across a ship he did not recognize. He called for the ship to identify itself, but he got no reply. He threatened to fire on the unidentified ship when a stranger called out angrily, "This is His Britannic Majesty's ship *Donegal,* 84 guns, Sir Richard Strachan, an English commodore [commanding]. Send your boat aboard!" This is a demand a superior ship would make of an inferior one—to send a small boat aboard so the captain could give whatever reprimand or orders he felt were necessary.

Preble, however, was unmoved. "This is the United States' ship *Constitution,* 44 guns, Edward Preble, an American commodore [commanding], who will be damned before he sends his boat on board of any vessel! Blow your

Edward Preble became commodore of the U.S. squadron that patrolled the Barbary States. His service aboard the *Constitution* was so successful that his sailors became known as "Preble's Boys."

The **Strait of Gibraltar** is a narrow body of water between Spain and Morocco.

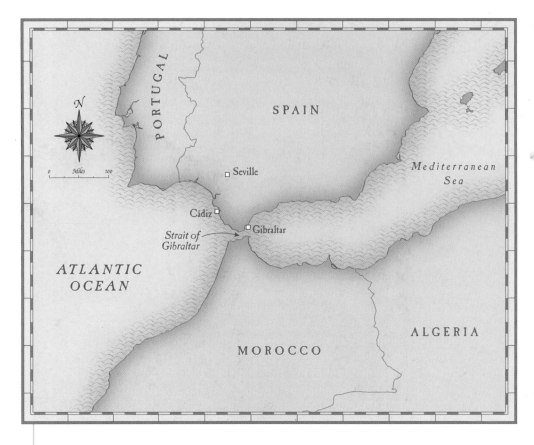

matches, boys!" he called, ordering his gunners to prepare to fire. The captain of the other ship, which turned out to be a smaller British frigate, immediately backed down and apologized. Preble's crew was impressed. Until then, they were unsure of him, and did not really respect him. Now that he had shown he could not be intimidated, they were proud of their new nickname, "Preble's Boys."

As the *Constitution* began to patrol the Mediterranean, things in the region were not going well. The U.S. ship *Philadelphia* was captured by a Moroccan ship. This act violated the treaty with Algiers. Preble sailed the *Constitution* to Morocco, as a show of force, and the Moroccan leader

* * * *

agreed to give the ship back. Unfortunately, the *Philadel-phia* was soon taken again, this time by Tripoli. Preble organized a naval attack to force its release, and the bombardment of Tripoli began. Preble led a naval artillery exchange with Tripoli's navy and cannons on the shore that lasted for days. Both sides suffered losses, but a peace agreement was eventually signed in the captain's cabin of the *Constitution*.

THE WAR OF 1812— THE GREAT CHASE

The War of 1812 presented another opportunity for the *Constitution* to demonstrate its extraordinary abilities. In fact, it was in this war that it would finally earn its famous nickname.

France's ruler, Napoleon Bonaparte, had always dreamed of conquering England; but the English navy was so powerful, it could stop any French invasion. Instead, he tried to destroy British trade by having his navy block Britain's entry into many important ports. Britain began doing the same to France. Soon it became dangerous for anyone to sail, and this hurt American shipping. Then the British began harassing any ships they believed were doing business with France. British ships, which were always short of sailors, were also kidnapping American sailors and forcing them into service in the British navy. The U.S. knew that it had to

THE SHIP'S GUNS—HOW BIG AND HOW FAR

The *Constitution's* guns were not all the same size. Smoothbore cannons are classified by the weight of the ordnance they fire. A 24-pounder fires a ball-shaped lead projectile that weighs 24 pounds (10.9 kilograms). The *Constitution* generally carried twenty 32-pounders and thirty-two 24-pounders. Some were special "long guns," designed for long-range firing—up to 1,200 yards (1,097 m), or more than two-thirds of a mile.

29

stand up against Britain, but it also knew that the British were superior on the seas. Instead of battling them there, the United States attacked their North American interests in Canada. The United States's decision to go to war with the more powerful Britain was a bold move and eventually established the new country as a military force.

The *Constitution* joined the war late. It had been in for repairs and was recruiting new crewmen. It left from Maryland on July 16, 1812, and headed for New York.

The Battle of New Orleans was the last of the War of 1812 and established the United States as a nation capable of defeating the most powerful armies and navies in the world.

Immediately it encountered a group of five ships. The new captain, Isaac Hull, who had been one of Preble's boys, thought they were American. They were not.

He realized his mistake at the last moment, but the winds died. The *Constitution* was just out of range of the guns of five British ships, and its sails were useless. From time to time, the British would fire to see if the American ship was close enough to hit. Hull knew that if the British got close, the *Constitution* could be destroyed. He had to find a way to put space between the *Constitution* and the enemy.

The crew used two difficult maneuvers to stay ahead of the British in what turned out to be thirty-six hours of calm seas. The first was what sailors call the "white ash breeze," named for the wood used to build rowboats. Several sailors rowed in front of the *Constitution* with towlines. For hours they rowed, trying to pull the huge ship to safety. Then the executive officer suggested a maneuver called "kedging." The ship's anchor, which weighed about 700 pounds (318 kg), was placed in a boat, carried ahead of the ship, and dropped in the water. Then the crew pulled the cable attached to the anchor, inching the ship forward. It was backbreaking work, but it proved to be successful. When the winds came up, the *Constitution* was far enough ahead to sail to safety.

Captain Isaac Hull, who had been one of Preble's Boys, was captain of the *Constitution* during many of its most famous sea battles.

IMPRESSMENT

British sailors often deserted. Sometimes they then went to work on American ships, which infuriated the British captains. The British began boarding foreign boats to take back their sailors. Then, they started "accidentally" capturing American-born sailors and forcing them to serve on British ships. Finally, they simply took whomever they wanted to fill out their crews, a practice called impressment.

Nineteenth-century sea battles were often fought until one of the ships was a ruined hulk. Sometimes the ship would be surrendered before it was destroyed and the victorious navy would add it to its fleet.

OLD IRONSIDES EARNS ITS NICKNAME

The *Constitution* entered the first of its most important battles on August 19, 1812. Captain Hull was cruising 700 miles (1,127 kilometers) east of Boston when he saw the HMS *Guerriere*, 44. The *Guerriere*, a British ship, was commanded by James Dacres, who knew that the *Constitution* was a superior vessel. However, he was used to British ships defeating anyone they encountered. In fact, Dacres had once boasted to the American commodore that he could defeat any of Humphreys' frigates. Now he would have his chance.

* * * *

Both ships prepared for battle, and the *Guerriere* passed the *Constitution* a number of times, firing **broadsides** as it did. Humphreys' design held, and the British cannonballs simply bounced off the sides. Seeing this, one of the crewmen is said to have called out, "Huzzah! Her sides are made of iron!" Forever after, the *Constitution* has been called "Old Ironsides."

Dacres held his course, and Hull rigged the sails for speed. He caught up to the *Guerriere*, getting as close as he could but patiently withholding fire. Finally Hull cried, "Pour in the whole broadside!" and all the starboard guns, loaded with rounds and **grapeshot,** let loose. Balls tore into the *Guerriere's* side, and the grape ripped through the sails and rigging. The *Guerriere* returned fire, with little effect. Its masts began to fall, and it slowed. The *Constitution* continued to fire, causing more devastating damage.

The two ships got so close that the **bowsprit** on the front of the *Guerriere* got caught in the *Constitution's* rigging. Both captains called for their crews to board the other, and the *Constitution's* **sharpshooters** killed and wounded many men. Even Dacres was wounded. The ships parted in the seas before any boarding could take place, and the rest of the *Guerriere's* masts fell over the sides. Helpless in the water, Dacres surrendered, and when the survivors were taken off the hulk, the British warship was burned. In all, fifteen men on the *Guerriere* were killed and sixty-three wounded. The *Constitution* lost seven men and had seven more hurt.

The proud British navy had sustained a terrible defeat that was far more costly than the price of a ship. Americans

WHY ARE SHIPS CALLED "SHE?"

While some people now consider it inappropriate, sailors have long called ships "she." It's been a tradition for so long that no one really knows how it got started. In many languages, words for non-living objects are either masculine or feminine. In most of those languages, modes of transport are female. Ships became referred to as "she." Another possible explanation is the close relationships the men had with their ships. Many captains are said to be "married" to the sea, or their ships.

33

had proven that the British navy was not invincible. It had been almost ten years since a British captain was forced to surrender. For Americans, it was a morale boost in a war that had not gone well. Many had been afraid that the United States would lose and have to surrender part of its territory to the British. Old Ironsides had won a very important victory indeed.

Several other American naval victories followed soon after. Then, in December 1812, it was once again the *Constitution's* turn. It was now under the command of

The *Constitution* carried more sails than any other ship, but when the winds died down, its crew would have to resort to many difficult maneuvers, such as towing, to get the ship moving.

* * * *

Commodore William Bainbridge (left) took the *Constitution* into battle against British Captain Henry Lambert's (right) *Java* in one of the hardest fought and most famous frigate battles in history.

Commodore William Bainbridge. The ship was patrolling near Brazil, protecting U.S. merchants. The *Constitution* came upon the HMS *Java*, 44, a British ship, with Captain Henry Lambert in command. What followed was one of the hardest fought frigate battles of all time.

The two ships were evenly matched, but the *Constitution's* crew was more experienced. They engaged and fired time after time. For two hours they circled, fired, rammed one another, and tried to blast holes in one another's sides. The *Java* had part of the bow shot away and one of its masts shot off. As it turned, it stopped, unable to get wind in its sails. The *Constitution* blasted the *Java* with a broadside. The *Java* tried to ram the *Constitution* but that just gave Old Ironsides a chance for another broadside. The *Java's* masts

35

In the mid-1800s, the *Constitution* was used as a training ship for cadets at the U.S. Naval Academy in Annapolis, Maryland.

came down, and its captain was killed. Finally the *Java* ceased firing and the *Constitution* backed away to make some repairs. Commodore Bainbridge was wounded twice but still in command. He positioned the *Constitution* with guns loaded toward the *Java*. The British crew surrendered. They sustained 122 casualties; the Americans, 34.

The U.S. Congress honored the victorious crew and captain. Congress was so impressed by the *Constitution's* performance in battle that it voted to expand the navy. American warships were still outnumbered. There were just too many British ships to defeat one by one, but the young country had proved it could build good ships and produce fine seamen. If the United States was going to be a world power, it would indeed need the kind of navy the *Constitution* had proved it could have.

RETIREMENT AND RENEWAL

The *Constitution*'s career was by no means over, but it had proved its worth. In 1815 it captured two more British warships. For the next dozen years, however, it was either in storage or on light duty in relatively peaceful waters. In 1828 the navy conducted a study to see how much it would cost to refurbish Constitution. It was widely reported that it would be too expensive to repair and that the *Constitution* would be destroyed.

When people heard that America's most famous fighting ship would be discarded like junk, the public reaction was immediate and emotional. Editorials in newspapers throughout the nation criticized the government as harshly as if it had ordered the death of a famous soldier. A twenty-one-year-old Harvard graduate named Oliver Wendell Holmes wrote a poem about the ship that became very popular. It suggested that such a great ship should have a better end. Better that it be sailed out to meet its own fate than to be taken apart, bit by bit. Instead, Congress voted to fix the *Constitution*.

Once repaired, the *Constitution* was put to many uses. Between 1835 and 1851 it served as flagship of several navy squadrons and **circumnavigated** the globe. It sailed the African coast looking for slave traders and served as a training ship at the U.S. Naval Academy. It even had to be hidden during the Civil War when Southerners threatened to destroy it as a symbol of Northern strength. The *Constitution* took its last foreign cruise in 1879. It even had a building built on top of it while it was used for storage.

Its poor condition and the quality of its service started

another public outcry in the late 1920s. The secretary of the navy initiated a "pennies" campaign among schoolchildren and patriotic groups to restore the *Constitution*. They raised $250,000, of which $31,000 came from U.S. servicemen. When its repairs were complete, the *Constitution* made a coast-to-coast tour of more than ninety ports, towed by a navy ship. It welcomed 4.5 million visitors to its decks. In 1934 it returned to Boston, eventually to serve out the rest of its life as a museum.

Another set of major repairs was begun in the early 1990s to prepare the *Constitution* for another milestone. In 1997, Old Ironsides sailed under its own power for the first time in 116 years to celebrate its bicentennial. As part of the celebration, a wreath was laid at the grave of its first captain, Samuel Nicholson.

The USS *Constitution* remains today the oldest commissioned ship in the U.S. Navy. The ship earned this honor for its unique service to the United States of America, helping the young country establish itself as a military power. Its design was flawless, allowing the ship to repel cannonballs as if it actually did have sides of iron. Its captains set the *Constitution* against the best ships the world had to offer and returned undefeated. It is this ship, Old Ironsides, that convinced the world, and even some in its own country, that the United States could hold its own with the strongest nations in the world.

Perhaps its old commander, Commodore William Bainbridge, said it best in 1831: "Never has she failed us. Her name is an inspiration. She was conceived in patriotism; gloriously has she shown her valor."

Oliver Wendell Holmes felt that the only way for the *Constitution* to be properly retired was in battle. His poem "Old Ironsides" is credited with saving the ship from destruction in 1830.

"OLD IRONSIDES"

by Oliver Wendell Holmes

September 16, 1830

Ay, tear her tattered ensign down!

Long has it waved on high,

And many an eye has danced to see

That banner in the sky;

Beneath it rung the battle shout,

And burst the cannon's roar;—

The meteor of the ocean air

Shall sweep the clouds no more.

Her deck, once red with heroes' blood,

Where knelt the vanquished foe,

When winds were hurrying o'er the flood,

And waves were white below,

No more shall feel the victor's tread,

Or know the conquered knee;—

The harpies of the shore shall pluck

The eagle of the sea!

Oh, better that her shattered bulk

Should sink beneath the wave;

Its thunders shook the mighty deep,

And there should be her grave;

Nail to the mast her holy flag,

Set every threadbare sail,

And give her to the god of storms,

The lightning and the gale.

In 1997, the *Constitution* left the dock under sail for the first time in 116 years. The ceremonies were part of the celebration of the 200th anniversary of the ship's launch.

Glossary

bowsprit—a large spar, like a pole, that projects forward from the front of a ship

broadside—mass firings of all the guns on one side of a ship

casting—something made in a mold, frequently from metal

circumnavigate—to sail completely around the world

consul—a government official representing his or her country in a foreign land

corsair—a Barbary pirate ship

cutwater—the front edge of a ship, which cuts through the water

despots—rulers with absolute authority

flagship—the ship that carries the commander of a fleet

grapeshot—a cluster of small iron balls fired together from a cannon

keel—the bottom of a ship

ordnance—supplies used as ammunition such as cannon
balls and gunpowder

piracy—robbery on the sea

privateers—armed private ships licensed to fight on
behalf of a particular country

rigging—the ropes and lines used aboard a ship, espe-
cially to work the sails

sharpshooter—someone trained to accurately shoot a
gun over a long distance

smoothbore—a cannon without grooves cut on the inside
of its barrel; the opposite of rifled

tributes—a fee paid to a country for protection or
safe passage

Timeline: Old Ironsides

1794

MARCH 27 Congress authorizes the building of six frigates to protect the U.S. merchant fleet. A Boston shipyard is awarded the contract to build the *Constitution.*

1797

OCTOBER 21 The *Constitution* is launched and christened on the third try, a month after two earlier attempts failed to move her more than 60 feet.

1798

JULY 22 The *Constitution* puts out to sea for the first time.

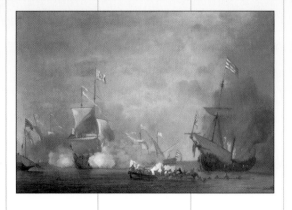

1798–1801

The *Constitution* sails in the West Indies to protect U.S. ships from French privateers, but sees no battle.

1803–1806

President Jefferson sends the *Constitution* to the Mediterranean to protect against Barbary pirates, and the ship takes part in bombardment of Tripoli.

JULY 17 Early in the War of 1812, the *Constitution* escapes five British ships through a series of legendary maneuvers.

1812

AUGUST 19 The *Constitution* defeats the *Guerriere* in the Atlantic Ocean, raising the perceived power of the U.S. Navy. In this battle it gains the nickname "Old Ironsides."

DECEMBER 29 The *Constitution* defeats *Java* off the coast of Brazil.

1813	1815	1828	1830	1897	1997
The *Constitution* returns to Boston and is blockaded for eight months by the British, finally slipping past them in December 1814.	**FEBRUARY 20** The *Constitution* captures the British ships *Cyane* and *Levant* off the island of Madeira.	The *Constitution* is declared unseaworthy and is scheduled to be destroyed.	 Oliver Wendell Holmes's poem "Old Ironsides" stirs emotions and popular support, and the ship is saved.	Boston celebrates the ship's centennial, and the *Constitution* goes on permanent display there.	**JULY 21** After years of repair, the *Constitution* sails under its own power for the first time in 116 years, just outside Boston Harbor.

45

To Find Out More

BOOKS

Gilmer, Thomas G. and William Gilkerson. *Old Ironsides*.
New York: McGraw-Hill, 1997.

Weitzman, David. *Old Ironsides: America Builds a Fighting Ship*.
Boston: Houghton Mifflin, 1997.

Young, Robert. *A Personal Tour of Old Ironsides*. New York:
Lerner Publishing Group, 2000.

ORGANIZATIONS AND ONLINE SITES

Naval Historical Center
Detachment Boston
Building 24 Maintenance and Repair
Boston National Historical Park
Charlestown Navy Yard
Boston, MA 02129

The USS Constitution Museum
www.ussconstitutionmuseum.org
The page specific to Old Ironsides is:
www.history.navy.mil/war1812/const1.htm

USS Constitution Web Page
www.ussconstitution.com

Index

Bold numbers indicate illustrations.

About the Author

Roger Wachtel has been an educator for sixteen years, first as a high school English teacher, then as a university instructor. He is now the writing specialist for the Peru Community Schools in Peru, Indiana. He was born in New Jersey, went to high school in Belgium, and now lives in Westfield, Indiana. He is married to Jeanette and has three sons, Thomas, Ben, and Josh. He has a Master's degree in English Education from Butler University. In his spare time, he reads and writes, follows the New York Mets passionately, and goes to automobile races with his sons and brothers. Roger is the author of another Cornerstones of Freedom book, *The Medal of Honor.*